Jamal and the Jade Soup

Text and illustrations by Terry T. Waltz

Jamal and the Jade Soup

Text and illustrations by Terry T. Waltz

ISBN-13: 978-1-946626-60-8
Published by Squid For Brains
Albany, NY
www.squidforbrains.com

Copyright ©2019 by Terry T. Waltz. All rights reserved. No part of this book may be reproduced or transmitted in any form or by any means, electronic or mechanical, including photocopying, recording or by any information storage or retrieval system, including with the intent to display it simultaneously to a larger audience, without the express prior written permission of the copyright holder.

This is Jamal. Jamal is a panda.

Jamal doesn't like hamburgers. He doesn't like tacos. He doesn't even like pizza!

Jamal only likes soup.

But Jamal has a problem. He doesn't have any soup. He is very hungry, but he doesn't have any soup to eat.

Jamal has no soup, but he has a piece of jade.
And he has an idea!

Jamal goes to see his friend Enzo.

Enzo says, "I don't have any soup."

Jamal says, "That's okay. I have a piece of jade. We can make jade soup!"

Jamal says, "Well, jade soup isn't bad. But jade soup with *peanut butter* is really good! Too bad we don't have any peanut butter!"

Enzo says, "Really? I have some peanut butter!"

Jamal says, "Good!"

And he adds Enzo's peanut butter to the soup.

Jamal says,
"Be careful! It's hot!"

Enzo says, "Not bad!"

Jamal says, "Jade soup with peanut butter is pretty good. But jade soup with peanut butter and a *sandwich* is even better! Too bad we don't have a sandwich."

Enzo says, "Look, there's A-San! Maybe A-san has a sandwich to add to the soup."

Jamal and Enzo say, "Hi, A-San. How are you? Long time no see! We have jade and peanut butter soup. Would you like to have some jade and peanut butter soup?"

A-San asks, "Is jade and peanut butter soup good?

Jamal says, "It's not bad, but jade and peanut butter soup *with a sandwich* is better. Too bad we don't have a sandwich."

A-San says, "I have a sandwich! Let's add my sandwich to the soup!"

So Jamal adds A-San's sandwich to the soup.

Jamal says, "Yes, jade and peanut butter and sandwich soup is pretty good. But jade and peanut butter and sandwich and *ketchup* soup is better! Too bad we don't have some ketchup!"

Bordon Cramsie, the famous chef, sees Jamal and Enzo and A-San.

Bordon Cramsie says, "Hi, guys! I have some ketchup. Jade soup and peanut butter and sandwich soup is good, but you are right. Jade and peanut butter and sandwich and *ketchup* soup is better! Let's add my ketchup to your jade and peanut butter and sandwich soup!"

So Jamal adds the ketchup to the soup. "It's really good!" say A-San and Enzo. "Not bad!" says Bordon Cramsie. "Not better than my soup, but not bad!"

One friend adds tortillas. Another friend adds cheese. Other friends add soy sauce and carrots and Chinese dumplings.

Everyone is happy, because they have lots of good soup to eat.

But Jamal is not happy. He is angry!

Unique words in order of appearance

this (1)
is (16)
Jamal (23)
a (20)
panda (1)
doesn't (5)
like (5)
hamburgers (1)
he (9)
tacos (1)
even (2)
pizza (1)
only (1)
likes (1)
soup (31)
but (10)
has (6)
problem (1)
have (14)
any (4)
very (1)
hungry (1)
to (12)
eat (3)
no (3)
piece (3)
of (6)
jade (17)
and (28)

an (1)
idea (1)
too (5)
goes (1)
see (3)
his (2)
friend (3)
hi (4)
how (2)
are (3)
you (5)
long (2)
time (2)
do (1)
want (1)
says (18)
I (5)
don't (5)
that's (2)
okay (1)
we (6)
can (1)
make (1)
well (1)
isn't (1)
bad (10)
with (4)
peanut (15)
butter (15)

really (4)
good (10)
some (4)
adds (5)
the (9)
be (3)
careful (3)
it's (7)
hot (3)
not (7)
pretty (3)
sandwich (14)
better (5)
look (1)
there (2)
maybe (1)
add (4)
say (2)
would (1)
asks (1)
let (2)
my (4)
so (2)
yes (1)
ketchup (6)
famous (1)
chef (1)
sees (1)
guys (1)

right (1)
your (1)
than (1)
lots (2)
friends (3)
all (1)
one (1)
tortillas (1)
another (1)
cheese (1)
other (1)
soy (1)
sauce (1)
carrots (1)
Chinese (1)
dumplings (1)
everyone (2)
eats (1)
happy (2)
because (1)
they (1)
angry (1)
ouch (1)
tooth (1)
in (1)

(Numbers in parentheses indicate how many times the word appears.)

www.ingramcontent.com/pod-product-compliance
Lightning Source LLC
Chambersburg PA
CBHW051351110526
44591CB00025B/2969